Where does Jesus Live?

Written by Peter Dill
Illustrations by Maria C. Martinez

- Backseat Media -

At Backseat Media, our mission is to create valuable resources that support families on their journey of faith. We're passionate about equipping parents and children with tools to encounter Christ in everyday life—cultivating a deep, lasting love for the faith that grows together as a family

Dad reads the Bible,
and mom sings a song.
We say His name often
as we all pray along.

But I still wonder
the answer He'd give.
I've asked my whole family:
Where does Jesus live?

We learn at church that
from Heaven He came.
We say in our seats,
"Holy is His name."

I still want to know
the answer He'd give.
In Heaven or earth:
Where does Jesus live?

My gramps loves Jesus,
and my grams does too.
They taught the whole family
each year as we grew.

But I keep thinking
the answer He'd give.
I really want to ask Him:
Jesus, where do you live?

I'll go to my room,
close my eyes in prayer.
I'll ask for an answer:
Jesus, are You there?

Lord, can I see You?
Will You please come here?
Where do You live, Lord?
Will You please appear?

Now that it's quiet,
as I open my eyes,
it's really You, Jesus!
Your whole body shines!

You point to my chest
and say it so clear:
"In your heart I will live
for all of your years."

"So tap on your heart,
and every time that you do,
it means I'm right here,
and My love is for you."

"This is your answer,
so now you'll always know:
I live in your heart,
come and say hello."

"Please never lose hope,
and never have fear.
I'm always right with you,
in your heart I'll be near."

The End

Coloring Pages

Thank you to everyone
who helped make this
book possible, especially
Tania and Clara.
Without your support and
belief in this vision, it could
not have been made.

Thank you to my babies who
inspire me every day to live up
to the honor of being your dad.
Thank you to the Lord, who
provides all good things.

- Peter Dill

www.ingramcontent.com/pod-product-compliance
Lightning Source LLC
Chambersburg PA
CBHW041800040426

42447CB00001B/34